DESI GUIDE TO CORPORATE SUCCESS

A personal guide for Indians by an Indian

By Soni Anand

Copyright © 2016 Soni Anand and CT Monell

ALL RIGHTS RESERVED. This book contains material protected under International and Federal Copyright Laws and Treaties. Any unauthorized reprint or use of this material is prohibited. No part of this book may be reproduced or transmitted in any form or by any means, electronic or mechanical, including photocopying, recording, or by any information storage and retrieval system without express written permission from the author.

Table of Contents

Introduction 5

Coming to America 6

Suit Up! 8

    Tips for looking your best in the corporate environment 8

    For guys 8

        Shirts 8

        Pants 9

        Shoes 9

        Jackets 9

        Upkeep 9

        Hygiene 10

    For Ladies 11

        Dresses 12

        Shoes 12

        Hygiene 13

        Makeup 13

        Grooming 14

    Food for thought 15

Speak Up! 16

    How to come across with authority on conference calls and meetings 16

        Never be silent 17

        Add to the conversation 17

        Ask Questions 18

        Speak up 18

Mute the phone 18

Email communication 18

Stand out! How to be an excellent performer. 19

Coffee Room and Water Cooler Etiquette 23

Vacation Time 26

Questions and Answers 29

Closing. 36

Introduction

Namaste.

I came to America from India when I was 19 and was abruptly introduced to the corporate world as soon as I got here.

I have observed a lot in my career regarding our culture and that's why I decided to write this book. I want to reach out to you and help you as a friend and mentor. Not everything in this book is for everyone. But if all of you can relate to at least one topic in this book and it helps you, I would be blessed that I made a decision to write this book.

Maybe some of you might say after reading this book, "Why should I care to invest in myself? I am here as a consultant on an H1-B visa. They hired me because I can deliver, not how I look or speak or am perceived. I just want to make my money and go back home and settle down there one day. This is not my home."

I completely understand because after more than 25 years, I still sometimes feel like this. However, you have to remember that working here is extremely competitive and if you want to do the best you can, there are some simple ways you can get the best results for you and your family.

As a friend, I humbly request you all to keep an open mind while reading this information.

Special thanks to CT Monell, an executive friend of mine who helped write the Q&A at the end of this book.

Anyone can benefit from reading this book. It is not just for those of us who were born in India. This book is to help us all excel at our work place. So Good Luck and keep reading...

Coming to America

I was overwhelmed with the first exposure I got to the corporate world. Like most of you probably are, I was a very shy, scared and demure person. I was quiet in meetings and on conference calls. I was always thinking to myself, "I do not belong here". It felt as if there was too much politics in this unfamiliar corporate world. I often felt misunderstood by my colleagues and co-workers.

We know the Western culture is very different from ours and it sometimes works against us. I started to notice that those of us born and raised in India had similar traits that have worked against us. For example, we address elders as "Uncle or Aunty" whereby in Corporate America we are told to address them by their first name or a nickname (I did not know that Bob could mean Robert, as an example!). We were always told to respect our elders and never argue with them. The same principle did not apply in the corporate world here. People argued with their elders and disrespected their bosses.

This scared me a little, to be truthful it scared me a lot. I remember crying in the subway train on my way home. I was overshadowed at work by some people who seemed to be just talkers and not doers. They were very influential by just using words and not by their skills or accomplishments. I was a doer, which means I like to do my job and deliver on projects without being told much what to do. For this reason I am very proud to be an Indian. We work hard and we deliver when asked to.

Besides calling elders by name, I noticed many of my Western colleagues had no problem saying "No" to the boss. I remember hearing the boss asking my co-workers if they had time to take on a new project. They always seemed to have an answer ready "I am so busy. I cannot get to it right now. I am completely buried right now" (yet they left at 5pm on the dot..hmmm). Sure enough, the boss' next stop would be my cube. I could never say "No" in the beginning and noticed that I was getting stuck with a lot more work than others.

We as a rule, often do not know how to say "No". We think by saying "No" we will upset the boss or he may think negatively about us. I have changed a lot over the years and one thing I learned to do is sound and look busy. If you don't look busy then people assume you have nothing to do. They don't think you are efficient and able to get all your work done on time, they assume you just don't have enough to do. I found that some of my colleagues were able to do this very well and never got asked to do more.

I was also shocked and upset to learn how our people were portrayed in movies and on TV. I learned that in the West, we were not always thought of in a positive light. I was told we smell of food or body odor, that we have odd styles of dress and that we could never be successful in the competitive corporate world. We would always be worker bees who have one foot out the door pointing to the East.

I spent a lot of time thinking about why this is so. I hope to address some of these things in the next few chapters.

At the end of the book I have a few common questions and answers that will help you move up the ladder in your company.

Suit Up!
Tips for looking your best in the corporate environment

Some of you may get offended by reading this chapter but this chapter or book is not to written to make you feel bad. This chapter is written to bring awareness to the things that we can do to shine at our workplace.

The name of the game here is to make you all feel confident in your workplace (and that carries on in real life as well).

The most important thing you can do is to invest in yourself.

For guys

Shirts

Gentlemen, you need to wear shirts that fit your body well. Don't pay attention to the size marked on the label, try the clothes on and make sure they look good on you.

Choose solid color shirts. In the corporate world solid or stripe shirts speak professionalism. Please do not wear printed shirts to work. You should have multiples of white and blue solid shirt in your closet. You can never go wrong with these colors.

If you do feel the need to buy stripes, then this is the rule: If you want to look taller in life you need to buy shirts with vertical stripes. Please do not buy shirts with horizontal stripes as it will make you look wider than you are.

If you want checkered shirts, my recommendation is to buy shirts with very small checks. Small checkered shirts will make you appear leaner.

Pants

Purchase two or three nice fitting pants. Please do not wear clothes that you bought from back home. The fashion sense in the Western corporate world is quite different from what we are used to at home. You need to buy straight cut docker pants with no pleats in the front. You should have at least one black pant, one navy blue pant and one beige (or khakhi pants as we call it) pant in your closet.

Any blue or white solid color shirt will go with your black or navy blue pants.

Shoes

Every man should go and invest in a nice pair of black and brown dress shoes. Please do not wear white socks with black or brown shoes. White socks should be reserved for your sneakers.

Wear black socks with your black shoes and brown socks with brown shoes.

Jackets

Wear a sports coat if you are making a presentation or meeting customers. A sports coat makes a good impression and gives the appearance of having confidence and authority.

Upkeep

Make sure that your shirts and pants are ironed. Please do not wear wrinkled clothes to work. Wrinkled clothes make other people think that you are lazy and you have no time to spend on yourself.

Observe how people who are in management positions dress. You will rarely see senior management wearing wrinkled clothes. The secret is that all the higher level management people invest in themselves. For example, they will give their shirts to laundromats to be dry cleaned or laundered. There are laundromats in your neighborhood that will launder your shirts for about a dollar.

If you buy expensive shirts, you can wear them multiple times before laundering them. The trick is you need to air them out. When you get home you need to hang your shirts so that can be refreshed. Do not throw your clothes carelessly on the bed or the floor.

Always wear an undershirt. This is necessary to avoid any sweat being shown on your shirt and also important because you do not want your chest hair to be seen. Although you might be told that chest hair is manly, it is not perceived that way in the Western world.

When choosing an undershirt, choose a round collar not a "V" style.

Hygiene

I cannot emphasize enough that everyone should be using a deodorant after bath. You have to use deodorant under your arms. Using deodorant should be like Mantra for everyone.

One cannot smell his own sweat and no one close will tell you. Body odor is one of the worse things to walk around with all day. People will be uncomfortable to work with you and will try to avoid you. Even worse, they may make fun of you behind your back.

I have experienced it myself. One day I went over to my coworker's cube and she was spraying febreze in her cube and wiping the seat with Lysol wipes. I asked her why she was doing that and she told me that a particular consultant was in her cube and he had body odor and that she needed to spray her cube to get the smell out. In this example, the consultant was not from our country, but we should still make sure that no one can say this about us.

You need to shower every morning, put on deodorant, wear a clean undershirt and undergarment and put on a well ironed shirt and pant. Do not substitute talcum powder for deodorant.

Use cologne sparingly. Comb your hair put a little gel or mousse to give it a nice touch.

Please do not put oil in your hair on weekdays. Oil has a smell that we all have gotten used to since childhood but people at work notice. We all have used coconut oil all through our lives and it does carry a smell. Please refrain from using coconut oil during the week.

Repeat! NO OIL in your hair during weekdays. Oil your hair as much as you want on weekends.

Wash your hair and apply gel or mousse.

Some of us are still bringing clothes from home. Some of you might think, "Why buy new clothes? I have my clothes stitched by my tailor". The bottom line is you need to invest a little in yourself. This investment will make you blend in at work. Unfortunately many people in corporate environments dislike people who look different. Things are changing with diversity programs at work, but the reality is that things still haven't changed a lot.

It is always said that first impression lasts long. You need to make an impression everyday as you never know who you might meet.

For Ladies

In my career I have observed generally there are two types of women. There are those who are pant driven which means they are more comfortable wearing pants and tops and then there are those who are dress driven and love to wear dresses or skirts. Which one are you? It does not matter because we all are going shopping!

As a woman you first need to be very comfortable with yourself. You have to spend some time to find out what size you really are. We as women tend to wear clothes smaller than we think we are and some women will buy clothes bigger than they are to hide their bodies. When you go shopping there are 2 sizing charts in clothes. Some are small, medium, large etc. and some sizes are in numbers such as 2, 4, 6, 8 etc.

If you are new to this western world the sizing numbers can be confusing. Small, medium and large is what we can understand and relate to better that the sizing in numbers.

One mistake we as busy women make is that we do not try on the clothes before buying them. When you are ready to buy something, pick a size smaller and larger and pick the one that makes you look and feel better. Don't get stuck on the size or the number. If you have to go a size bigger than you are in clothes, it is OK. All clothes are cut differently. If you cannot decide then go shopping with a friend. It always helps to have another opinion or perspective.

For work, choose plain pants with nice printed or solid tops. This works best for women.

Dresses

Dresses or skirts should not be short. The best dress/skirt length is knee length with a nice pair of dress heels.

Shoes

Buy a good pair of dress heels. Try them on to make sure they are comfortable enough for you to wear them all day. They do not have to be high heels if you are not comfortable in them.

Get a nude and a black heel as these will go with every color dress or pants that you wear. Please do not wear slippers that you brought from India to work.

Hygiene

Refer to the guys section on this topic as it contains the same advice for women.

Use a deodorant after you shower. Do not substitute talcum powder for deodorant. Use a perfume after you dress up for the day for an extra boost.

Makeup

Don't overdo makeup for work. Simple and basic is best. Use a moisturizer every morning after your bath.

Try a little bit of foundation or face powder, it will do wonders to perk up your complexion.

The biggest challenge that you might have is matching the foundation shades to your skin color. Try going to beauty counters in the big shopping malls and ask the person for advice. Keep asking until you find the right shade for you. Sometimes it takes a little bit of experimenting and asking people for help.

Use a light brown or light pink lipstick. Please do not wear reds or maroons to work. Apply a mascara to highlight your eyes. If you do not want to apply mascara on your eyes then kajal pencil will be just fine.

I know most of you women out there are saying, "Who has time for all this? There is so much going on in the mornings. Getting kids ready for school or daycare, getting breakfast ready, lunch boxes ready for work, it's a miracle that I can even get to work on time".

I completely understand your concerns because I have been there. But one thing that I've learned is that adjusting to the corporate world is necessary. All these things will become a part of your routine once you start using them. This does not take too much time and will enhance your beauty and confidence at work.

Grooming

In the winter toe nails do not matter as you will be wearing closed shoes. But in the summer, make sure that your nails are cut and that you have a nail polish on them.

In the summertime we all wear open shoes and feet look really bad if you have nail polish that is all worn out. The same goes for your hand nails. Apply a light color nail polish to make your hands look good. Refrain from dark colors like maroon because when they chip (and they will), it will look unpleasant.

People notice everything at work. In our community we do a lot of cooking and we are constantly washing and cleaning. There is less chance for our hands to be looking great all the time. That's the reason I mentioned a light pink nail polish or a nude color nail polish. If the light color nail polish wears off during the week, it is less likely to draw attention. If you put dark nail polish and it wears off, it really looks bad.

Please keep a hand cream with you at all times.

Apply the hand cream all over your hands, legs and feet. Hands, legs and feet get very dry and with our skin tone it looks bad. Applying a little cream all over your hands, legs, feet and arms will give it a smooth look all throughout the day.

If you get a perfumed hand and body lotion even better, you will be smelling nice all day.

All these tips mentioned will help you not only in the corporate world but also in everyday life.

Food for thought

One very important thing that we do not realize is the food smell in our clothes. When we cook in our home we need to make sure that our jackets and clothes are in our closet as far away as possible from the kitchen. Close your closet door and then your bedroom door when you are cooking.

This is very important if you are living in a small apartment. If your clothes are lying everywhere, they will absorb the cooking smells.

We get so accustomed to the food smells in our lives that we do not realize that our clothes are smelling of food. Clothes smelling of food is as bad as body odor for the corporate world.

Do not cook food after you are dressed for work. If you have to cook in the morning, the routine should be: Cook, shower and then dress up.

Desi people are often described as people who always smell of food and spices. So please make sure to pay close attention to everything in this chapter. Invest in good clothes, shoes, hair products and cologne. But remember, everything will be a waste if you end up smelling like food.

Speak Up!
How to come across with authority on conference calls and meetings

Conference calls are a big part of corporate life. It connects people across the globe to share information and solve problems. It is quite common for people to speak for years but never actually meet face to face in big companies.

For our culture, conference calls sometimes work against us. Because we can't see the other people on the line, we have to make sure our words and our tone comes across effectively. It is very important to understand that there is much diversity in culture and world view amongst the people attending these calls.

The famous author Malcolm Gladwell highlighted an interesting issue in one of his books. He said at one time, Korean Air was suffering from more plane accidents than other airlines despite having the same equipment. After a study was done attempting to understand why Korean Air had so many accidents, it was determined that the problem was due to "culture". It seems that especially in Korean culture one is taught not to question authority. If someone speaks up, it is considered rude or rebellious. Because people are taught to value passive following of orders, they would not speak up when the pilot was making errors resulting in accidents and other mishaps.

There is also another story of a Colombian pilot who ran out of fuel because air traffic control kept postponing his landing. A comment was made that no American pilot would allow the plane to run out of fuel because the culture values speaking up.

We should learn an important lesson from this. We should put our cultural values aside a moment and remember we are on a conference call with people from other cultures who are perceiving us in ways we may not agree with. We want to put our best face on a conference call. In order to do so, we must keep the following in mind.

Never be silent

One of the most common criticisms of our people is that we are too quiet. If you are invited to a conference call and do not say one word, people assume you are not listening or not interested. They also will assume you are not "on the ball". This is probably one of the biggest reasons why we are overlooked in the corporate world.

Always make a point to say something and have your voice heard. It may seem to you that many people on the call are just talking to be heard, but there is value in doing that. Don't sit silently, make sure your thoughts, ideas, contributions and questions are heard by everyone. Speak a little slower and more clearly on a call too.

Add to the conversation

It is very difficult for us to contradict our bosses or other authority figures. One way to add a different viewpoint without sounding contradictory is to say "Yes and...". This way it sounds like you agree with what the person said, but you are adding another viewpoint.

You can also say, "You bring up a very important point AND we should ..."

Always validate what people are saying and they will be more open to your ideas.

Ask Questions
Don't be afraid to ask questions. If you have a question or don't understand something, chances are that other people on the call have the same question but are afraid to ask. However, don't ask too many questions, it's a delicate balance. Use questions to clarify points and to move the conversation forward. If you want to know more but don't want to detract from the call, say "I have a question but I will take it offline with you."

Speak up
A common criticism of us is that we speak very softly or mumble. Please be sure to speak clearly and increase your volume. This is very important to do on conference calls so that people can hear you.

Mute the phone
Remember to mute your phone when you are not speaking. Background noise is very distracting on the call. When you are working from home and have kids and pets, make sure your phone is muted when you are not talking. If you are the person who is adding the background noise, it will reflect poorly on you.

Email communication
Be aware that there are some unique phrases said by people from India that could take away from your message. For example, many people in India, when asking for a favor, will write, "Please do the needful". This is a common phrase, but be aware that this is not proper American English. If you write that you will be automatically be considered an outsider. Try to use the phrases that Americans use or the people in the country you are working in. In America, just say "Please" or "Thank you". Simple communication is best.

Stand out! How to be an excellent performer.

In this chapter I will reveal the secrets to standing out at work, getting a great rating and hence a bigger raise and bonus.

Most big companies have a way of managing employee performance. There is only one pot of money to distribute for raises and bonuses every year. How do organizations distribute this money? By what they call "differentiating" the great employees from the good and not so good employees. Every company has a unique way of ranking their people, but the principles behind getting the best ranking are usually the same.

I will give you some insight into how it works. At the beginning of the year, your boss will give you goals that you need to accomplish for the year. Of course throughout the year you will be asked to do more than these goals, but the ones that are written down in the system are the ones used to track your performance and are the most important. It doesn't matter if you work hard all year round. If your boss gave you a goal, for example, to minimize errors on your databases by 50%, it doesn't matter if you had 15 successful projects and missed this goal for the year. You will be evaluated on how well you did to reduce the errors not so much the 15 successful projects.

So, the first secret is to make sure the goals your boss records for you are realistic and achievable. You also must realize that these are the most important for you to pay attention to because these goals will determine your raise and bonus next year.

All ranking systems are based on the bell curve, meaning most employees will be in the middle. Some systems call being in the middle, "meets expectation" or "valuable employee". If you show up to work, do your job and don't cause any problems, you will probably be in this rating.

If you have trouble doing your job because you don't have the right skills or you are distracted by personal issues, you might be in the bottom of the curve called "needs improvement". Many companies will fire people who "need improvement" so you never want to be in this level. Make sure you have the right skills for your job and by continuing to read this chapter, you will be a top performer.

Let's recap: Pay attention to the goals you are given at the beginning of the year and make sure you have a plan to achieve them because how you achieve these goals will be a big part of your rating for the year. Do not lose track of your goals by all the other projects you are given.

The next secret is to make sure your goals have a way to measure them. For example, if your boss says to reduce database errors by 50%, try to exceed that amount by reducing 60, 70 or even 100%. If you have a yardstick to measure all your goals, you can also show how you exceed your goals. If you exceed your goals, you will have to be rated very well by your boss. There is no denying that you did well if you can show objectively that you exceeded your goals.

To get to the next level, you have to exceed your goals and do even greater. Remember, this is not so much about working hard, but working smart. Using the example above, if your goal is to reduce database errors by 50% but you spent your whole year working on projects and forgot this goal, you worked hard but not smart. To work smart, you must do a great job with your goal.

For example, if you reduce your database errors by more than 50% and then come up with standard methods your colleagues can use to reduce errors on their databases, you not only exceeded your goal but you went above and beyond. Leadership in corporations are looking for people who can do this. Going beyond your area of responsibility is what makes you a great employee, not just a good employee. I will give you more examples, because this is a very important secret to learn so that you can stand out.

Whenever you do something great for your team or yourself, think about how you can help other teams, departments and colleagues do the same. This is a very important part of your ranking.

Many people don't realize that even though you surpassed your goals and your manager thinks you are great, you could still get a bad rating. I will tell you why.

After your manager submits your rating in the system, he or she will have to meet with other managers and defend why you got your ranking. If there are employees in other groups that also did well, their managers have to argue and fight among themselves to distribute the rankings in the bell curve. For example, if Donna has 5 employees and Tom has 5 employees, there can only be a few great employees and there must be a couple "needs improvement" employees who will eventually get fired.

In this example, Donna and Tom are not allowed to say all their employees are great. This is why it's important for you to show you exceeded your goals and went above and beyond by making your success visible to other managers and departments.

If you work for Donna and you were able to help Tom's team be successful, when Donna and Tom meet to determine ratings,

Tom will be more inclined to give you the great rating if he knew who you were and you helped his team. If Tom had a negative experience with you or sees you spending too much time in the coffee room or coming in late, he will not agree with giving you a great rating. Remember, perception is everything and all managers have input in how well you do in the company.

This is why it's important to know how the rating system works. If you just come to work, do your job and go home and nobody knows who you are, you will never get the great rating. Worse, because you don't do anything extra, you could be given the bad rating and eventually get fired.

Let's summarize. Pay attention to your goals, exceed them and go beyond your team and department to help them be successful. Be seen. Volunteer for assignments instead of waiting to get them from your bosses.

Follow these steps and you will get a great rating and make the most money you can.

Coffee Room and Water Cooler Etiquette

Working in the corporate world for many years, the following has been my observation. I have been guilty of doing this, but I have changed and am very careful of not repeating these mistakes.

We tend to cling on to our own kind in the corporate world. And I can truly understand why. We do not have much in common with many Westerners. To some extent we are afraid to talk in front of them. It's difficult to have conversations with them since we were not born here and we did not share the same experiences with them growing up. They like to talk about games, TV series and activities that we cannot relate to.

Since we are so far away from our country, we find comfort in hanging out with our own kind. We can talk in our own language, we can discuss Bollywood movies and cricket matches. We become friends with the desi people at work and we start inviting them home and build a friendship.

Everything is good given our culture. But the Westerners sometimes do not view it that way. They think that the Desi are always talking in their own language and they consider it a big disrespect to them in the workplace.

Indians tend to form a group and they will always go to get coffee together, eat lunches together and even take walks together at work.

Eating lunches is fine as it is in the cafeteria but we as a community need to be very mindful of how we behave in the coffee area or kitchen area if your office has one. The water cooler area is included in this discussion as well. Please do not hang out in these areas and speak in your native language. There is no need to do that at work.

In one place I worked, there were two main groups of people from our community; a women's group and a guy's group. Each group varied from 4 to 8 people. Each of these groups religiously went to the coffee area between 9.30 am and 10 am and in the afternoon between 3 and 3.30pm.

They all used the corporate supplied milk which was in the refrigerator and which was meant for everyone to use just a little bit for their tea or coffee. However, our culture folks fill up their glasses with milk and heats them in the microwave for 2 - 3 minutes until the milk boils. We want to make instant coffee and that requires a lot of milk. I have been in the coffee room waiting while each member of the group take turns to heat up their milk (2 to 3 minutes each).

While they are heating the milk they all are talking loudly in their own language and socializing. This is not accepted well as people from other cultures get very upset about this. Taking up so much milk and hogging up the coffee room and the microwave for at least 20 to 30 minutes while the people from other culture have to wait is not a good scene. It came to the point that when people came to the coffee area and saw the Indian group congregating, they huffed and walked away.

This scenario is wrong on many levels. Firstly our community is perceived as drinking all the milk, taking up space in the kitchen every morning and evening, talking in our own language. This offends people from other cultures and they are under the false perception that we are talking about them.

We need to be mindful about this activity as we can damage the relationship with the people we work with. I spoke in my language once while there was another woman from my group who did not understand the language. Instantly she was offended and spread in the department that I was speaking bad about her and that's why I was talking in my language in front of her. My work relationship took a toll for the worse with her after that and it took a very long time to undo the damage.

So do your best to avoid going to coffee rooms or water cooler areas in large groups and avoid talking in your language in front of other people.

If you visit your fellow peers in their cubes and converse in your language, make sure you are speaking softly and try to make it quick in order for other communities not to pass judgement on you.

We are working abroad and we do need to be careful and respectful of their culture. We should never forget that we are not working in our country. We have to understand that our colleagues can be very offended and that they will rarely reveal what they feel to our face but will talk behind our backs about us.

In addition, by hanging out longer at the water cooler or coffee rooms in bunches of 5 or more gives an impression that we are not working and that we are enjoying and socializing. This perception will hurt you the most if you are a consultant. Be aware of your surroundings and mindful of your behavior at work. Don't let it be an everyday pattern.

This behavior may not apply to everyone but this is what I have noticed in my company.

Try and get coffee alone and get back to your desk so you are not perceived as the socializer instead of a contributor.

Vacation Time

Do not take long vacations.

Unlike many Europeans, Americans rarely ever take all 4 weeks of vacation time at once. They distribute these 4 weeks across the year. It works for them as they usually have their families nearby. So all their vacation time is vacationing with their families or when their kids are off from school. There are some who will take every Friday off as a vacation for a few months.

I wish this kind of vacation pattern could work for us. Wishful thinking! Because I got married and came to America, it meant that my parents and siblings were all in India almost 8000 miles away.

Because of the distance and travel expense, I had no choice but to take my 4 weeks of vacation at one time. If I was going to go to India and spend all that money on an airplane ticket then it better be for all 4 weeks. I remember my boss giving me a lot of trouble over this. "4 weeks is not allowed," he said. He complained that this means my colleagues in the group have to be bound by the systems I support for 4 weeks straight. My argument was "But I help out when they are on vacation." My boss countered, "Yes, you help out but it is one week when they are away not 4 weeks at a stretch".

He finally gave in and allowed me to take my vacations as the Human Resources department had to step in and explain that if an employee has time accumulated then they are entitled to take it.

What I did not realize in the beginning of my career was that taking 4 weeks at a stretch would not be received well by other team members. I would get subtle comments from other people indicating that they were very busy when I was gone and they had to take care of their systems as well as mine. I realized that my colleagues do not like us taking time off all at one stretch. They have to support our systems and also jump in on our projects.

I still take vacations home but have minimized it to 3 weeks. I do understand that we have to take time off but it does have a cost and an impact on our career. Some of you may be working in companies that have no issues with you all taking time off. For years I thought my promotion was impacted because I was out for a month. I also noticed that in my absence the people who filled in on my projects that I had worked so hard on…ended up taking credit for my work.

Even just recently, I had to go to India in November. I was working on 2 critical projects which were handed over to me in August. I completed one project successfully in October.

The other project had 3 phases. I completed 2 phases successfully by October. I asked my Team member to fill in for me when I was away in November for the last phase. When I came back I learned that he did nothing on my project since it wasn't priority for him. I had to scramble to get the project back on track but he got credit for the success of the last phase.

To add insult to injury, my company had a new reward system called "points" introduced in the summer. If you as a team member did a great job, your boss could allocate points to you and then based on those points you could buy nice items from a catalog.

So when I got back to work in the beginning of December, It was brought to my attention that my boss had allocated points to team members for their work efforts on my projects. I did not get a single point. I was annoyed and upset especially because my boss personally told me in October, before I left for India, that I did an excellent job on both the projects and that I made him look "GOLDEN" in front of his bosses. After being told this personally by my boss, I was upset not getting any points. So one day after a meeting I asked him if I could speak with him. I explained my concern to him and asked him why I was not awarded any points especially after he praised me on my projects. He looked at me and told me "I didn't give you any points? Are you sure. I could have sworn I did. Well Maybe because you were out the whole month of November. Oops, I guess out of sight out of mind". I just sat there and thought to myself really...out of sight out of mind is all he had to say? Was he really punishing me for the time I took time off?

I am not sure how your coworkers, bosses or company handles your time off but I am sure that at some point we all have gotten grief for being out for so long.

The purpose of this chapter was to make you all aware that even though we take long vacations it does come with a little setback at our work so please be mindful.

Questions and Answers

I work in Information Technology. How can I feel more valuable to the business?

Everyone in the IT organization should be held accountable for the success of the business. While most people may agree with this statement, very few in IT positions actually know how to do this. Learning how to be the business, instead of a cost center, can help bring IT organizations back to their priorities of helping the company increase revenue, lower costs and improve services. IT Operations and Support, which is often the heart and soul of the IT organizations needs to see itself as a front office asset.

Many large organizations see the IT group as separate and apart from the business. IT is seen as a service provider and not as a business partner, especially IT Operations and Support. For example, how does the Unix SA in a large organization, who is part of a central support team, know how he or she contributes to the value of the company's stock price, revenue or business strategy? After all, it isn't very clear. There are different reporting lines and IT groups are usually islands in the organization. IT people are seen as the 'geeks' in the corporation. A popular trend now is to move IT personnel and members of central support teams out of the way to 'non-money center' (less expensive) locations, far removed from the action. These displaced workers process service requests bound to an SLA and except for an occasional escalation, probably never hear from the businesses they support. The implication is that IT is a service provider that can be cut when necessity calls for leaner times.

You may be a lead or manager of one of these teams. How can you increase your business relevance? For example, imagine you were in an elevator with your company's Chief Executive. How would you answer the question, "How's everything going?" For IT people, the way to answer in business terms is not often very clear. For example, do you know how to translate your knowledge of servers, operating systems, middleware and processes into dollars? Are you able to speak and think in the language of your business? When I was first asked this question in this light it became clear to me that IT operations need help in this area.

I've found many IT people think things should be the other way around. They want the business to understand technology. They want to speak about bits and bytes to the business. They want the CEO to know about hypervisors and virtual storage. This happens when the IT organization grows so big that it begins to confuse the running of its operations as 'the business 'instead of the real business that it supports. This identity crisis is entirely normal and is a perfectly normal stage of evolution. Unfortunately, it's a stage where many IT organizations can become stuck. Projects are undertaken that have no relevance to the business goals. Managers review fancy charts and PowerPoint presentations with 'uptime' and response SLAs but don't know what the information means for the bottom line. IT support teams don't understand how what they do affects the business. Employees in these teams don't command the language and thought processes of the business. Because these orphan IT organizations get consumed by their own priorities and are unable to communicate their relevance, they are relegated to 'overhead'.

The good news is, understanding how to be part of the business is very simple. The most important thing to remember is that businesses are around for only one reason and that is to make money. The way a company makes money is by understanding and reducing its costs, improving services and managing risks.

Most businesses have a 'front office' and a 'back office'. The front office is the part of the business that is making money. This could be a sales team, a trading desk or even a programmer. These are the 'front line' or money makers of the firm. The 'back office' is the support teams, the overhead costs of the business. People in the front office are under a lot of pressure to perform. There is no question in their minds as to how they contribute to the business success. If they don't contribute within a certain amount of time, they will be gone. They will be replaced by someone who can. The front office knows exactly how much money it costs to run and knows exactly who is contributing and who is not. Most IT organizations don't feel this pressure. Sadly, they don't even know how they contribute to the success of the business. People in IT teams can flounder around for years, never understanding how to be part of the front office game.

So how can an IT organization become more business savvy? The first step is to speak and think in terms of the business. Know how much you spend and how much you cost. Remember businesses want to Increase Revenue, Avoid costs and Improve service (IRACIS) to stay competitive. Everything you do starting right now, should be increasing revenue, avoiding costs or improving service. If it's not, you should question why it's being done.

How can you help your company increase revenue? Well, for one by minimizing downtime. Keep the businesses you support running so they can be in the game making money. For example, every service request that sits without an acknowledgement or is waiting in a queue represent dollars of lost opportunity. If your group doesn't track a metric for how long these requests take to get completed, then start to do it. If you can find ways to reduce the waiting time of your business, you are increasing revenue! The best part is, you can show your boss or your business in tangible ways how you are making money—how you are part of the front office. When the company executive asks you how is everything, you can now say how much money you helped the company earn today.

Another way to help the company is by reducing its costs. Study your projects and initiatives to understand how to explain them in terms of money. A server consolidation project is not a VMWare implementation; it's a way to return three dollars for every dollar spent. Learn to prioritize your projects in terms of dollars and watch your overhead organization become business relevant.

Start speaking about your work in terms of dollars saved, dollars earned and opportunities exploited. Encourage your colleagues to do the same. Add a dollars perspective to your metrics reporting. Know how much your services cost. Understanding how you help the company make money and being able to speak its language will take you from back office to front office in no time.

I feel there is too much to do and my boss is too demanding. What can I do about this?

Can't Get Your Work Done? Someone else can. Times are tough for many companies as budgets are cut yet deliverables need to be met. It's normal for people to feel overworked and frustrated to do even "more with less".

I've encountered two types of people in my career. There are those who feel work can wait until they are ready to do it and there are those who continuously push themselves to find creative ways to get the work done. Which one are you?

I've actually heard an employee say to his boss when asked to do something, "I have to do A, B, C, D--which one do I need to drop?" His boss was not happy with that answer. The truth is, superstars in the organization find ways to get all the work done. If you find yourself disagreeing with this statement and offering excuse after excuse as to why management is uncaring or unreasonable, then you will find yourself out of a job. Why? Because no matter how hard management's expectations are, no matter how much you're asked to do, there is someone who doesn't feel the same way as you and can actually get all the work done and more! Perhaps your methods are outdated. Consider that someone knows how to do what you can't do cheaper, faster, and....better than you.

The lesson here is that 'No' is not really an option. It's not an option when the economy is bad, jobs are scarce and there are people who would love to have the job you have and the opportunity to get everything done.

How can I feel more appreciated at work?

I learned many years ago that we can influence others very subtly by carefully choosing the words we use. A big part of communication is saying things in the way that conveys the appropriate tone or produce the results that you want. The right word can get you the results you are seeking.

We often make fun of government officials who are very obvious when they use words to manipulate circumstances. One tip you can use in your day to day is as follows:

When you do a favor for someone or perform a service, many of us say colloquially "No problem" or "Don't worry about it". The appropriate response is, "You're welcome." Why? It goes back to our roots of surviving by working with others. "You scratch my back and I'll scratch yours." This is the law of reciprocity at work.

Wikipedia says the following:

"Reciprocity in social psychology refers to responding to a positive action with another positive action, rewarding kind actions."

When you say "No problem," you essentially and subtly leave the other person "off the hook". You just did something for them, they thanked you (now they owe you), but you just said "Don't worry about it." Additionally, by just saying "Don't worry about it, it's no problem," you also devalue the service you just performed. You just did something worthy of a, "Thank you", it's valuable!

In business, you want to leverage the law of reciprocity.

Try saying, "You're welcome. I know you would do the same for me." It may seem a bit uncomfortable for some of you to say this, but it's entirely normal. And in business, it's the difference between surviving and floundering. It's not being manipulative, it's using a fundamental law of survival in the workplace.

We need others to be successful. See your actions as part of an ecosystem of favors to achieve collective results in your organization.

How can I sound more competent at work?

It's important for people in corporations to display a sense of control and competence. One way to do this is by being very exact when providing information. Which answer sounds more competent?

Q: Can you tell me how many widgets you produce a day?
Person A: "We produce over 100 widgets per day."

Person B: "We produce an average of 103.7 widgets per day"

Person B sounds like she is on top of her game, fully aware of her important metrics. In fact, both answers are correct, but the manager that can be very specific sounds more in control.

Be aware of the subtle signals you send in your everyday answers.

Imagine if your company was bought by a rival organization and they are interviewing everyone for fit in the new firm. When companies merge, there are three lists created: a 'Retain' List, a 'Transition' List and a 'Cut' list. You can project a sense of competence and authority if you memorize some key statistics about your team or your specialty. If you are in Information Technology, for example, know how many Servers/Desktops/Applications you support. Know how many incidents are generated daily. In general, understand your key indicators and be able to spit out numbers. This will help make sure you are on the 'Retain' list.

Numbers convey authority and when you can speak about them with precision, you show that you are involved and leading in your organization.

People will also think you're smart.

Closing

 I would like to personally thank each and every one of you for taking the time to read this book. I hope I was able to guide you to enhance your career.

I wish each and every one of you the very best.

Namaste.

www.ingramcontent.com/pod-product-compliance
Lightning Source LLC
Chambersburg PA
CBHW041149180526
45159CB00002BB/756